T0114211

Health Information Management Handbook Series;

EHR Acronyms

Health Information Management Handbook Series; EHR Acronyms is an alphabetical compilation of Acronyms related to Health Information Management (HIM), the Electronic Health Record (EHR), Health Information Standards, Information Technology (IT), Telecommunications (TC) and Project Management (PM). The author has integrated common variations of terms into a single reference suitable for use by both students and working professionals within the health care industry.

Other Publications in the author's
 Health Information Handbook Series:

EHR Glossary, 2008

EHR Retention Schedules, (Coming Soon)

Order this book online at www.trafford.com/08-0563
or email orders@trafford.com

Most Trafford titles are also available at major online book retailers.

Note for Librarians: A cataloguing record for this book is available from Library
and Archives Canada at www.collectionscanada.ca/amicus/index-e.html

Cover Design/Artwork by Martin Stoutenburg
Creative(RF)#73782158/Getty Images©
Also published under: ISBN 978-0-9783454-3-3
e-HRM Consulting Inc.
e-Mail: ehrm@telus.net

Printed in the United States of America.

ISBN: 978-1-4251-7744-7 (sc)

www.trafford.com

North America & international
toll-free: 1 888 232 4444 (USA & Canada)
phone: 250 383 6864 ♦ fax: 250 383 6804
email: info@trafford.com

The United Kingdom & Europe
phone: +44 (0)1865 722 113 ♦ local rate: 0845 230 9601
facsimile: +44 (0)1865 722 868 ♦ email: info.uk@trafford.com

10 9 8 7 6 5 4 3 2

PREFACE

The *Health Information Management Handbook Series; EHR Acronyms* is a companion publication to the *Health Information Management Handbook Series; EHR Glossary* to support the clear communication of your ideas and strategies across health information and health care disciplines.

By no means is this list comprehensive. There are alternate clinical uses of acronyms and healthcare disciplines whose acronyms I have not included in this handbook in an attempt to remain grounded in information management related practices.

As in all industries, we strive for administrative speed and efficiency. In doing so, we have the potential to create a new acronym for whatever our current project may be. To assist you in your own environment, you will find a few lines at the end of each alphabetical split to complement this reference with your own frequently used acronyms.

Karanne

LEGEND: DOMAIN ACRONYMS & ABBREVIATIONS

ACRONYM or ABBREVIATION	DOMAIN
CL	Clinical
BUS	Business, general
HIM	Health Information Management
IM	Information Management
IT	Information Technology
LAW	Legal
ORG	Organizational Management
PM	Project Management
STD	Standards Development

ACRONYM	DEFINITION	DOMAIN
A		
AAMT	American Association of Medical Transcriptionists	ORG
AAHP	Association of Allied Health Professionals	ORG
ABC	Activity-Based Costing	HIM
ABC	Automatic Bandwidth Control	IT
AC	Actual Cost	PM
AC	Acute Care	CL
AC	Advisory Committee	ORG
ACAHO	Association of Canadian Academic Healthcare Organizations	ORG
ACC	Ambulatory Care Clinic	ORG
ACD	Automated Call Distribution	IT
ACGs	Adjusted Clinical Group (formerly Ambulatory Care Group)	HIM
ACG	Ambulatory Care Group (now Adjusted Clinical Group)	HIM
ACHE	American College of Health Executives	ORG
ACTH	Association of Canadian Teaching Hospitals	ORG

ACRONYM	DEFINITION	DOMAIN
AD	Address	IM
AD	Active Directory	IT
AD	Addendum Document (ISO)	STD
ADE	Adverse Drug Event	CL
ADF	Automated Document Feeder	IM
ADL	Activities of Daily Living	CL
ADT	Admission, Discharge, Transfer	HIM
ADT	Application Development Team	IT
AERS	Adverse Event Reporting System	HIM
AHA	Alberta Hospital Association	ORG
AHIMA	American Health Information Management Association	ORG
AHSCs	Academic Health Science Centres	ORG
AI	Archive Index	IM
AI	Artificial Intelligence	IT
AIA	Access to Information Act (Federal)	LAW
AIIM	The Association for Information and Image Management (ANSI)	ORG
AIMS	Abnormal Involuntary Movement Scale	CL

ACRONYM	DEFINITION	DOMAIN
AIMS	Administrative Information Management System	IT
AIMS	Automated Information Mapping Systems	IM
AIPPA	Access to Information and Protection of Privacy Act (Newfoundland & Labrador, Northwest Territories, Nunavut, Yukon)	LAW
AIS	Abbreviated Injury Scale	CL
AL	Assisted Living	CL
ALC	Alternate Level of Care	HIM
ALOS	Average Length of Stay	HIM
ALPHA	Association of Local Public Health Agencies (Ontario)	ORG
ALM	Application Life Cycle Management	IT
AMA	American Medical Association	ORG
AMA	Against Medical Advice	CL
AMIA	American Medical Information Association	ORG
AMRA	American Medical Record Association (now AHIMA)	ORG
ANI	Automatic Number Identification	IT
ANN	Artificial Neural Network	IT

ACRONYM	DEFINITION	DOMAIN
ANSI	American National Standards Institute	ORG
A/P	Accounts Payable	BUS
API	Application Program(ming) Interface	IT
AQAM	Association Québécoise des Archiviste Médicales	ORG
A/R	Accounts Receivable	BUS
AR	Attributable Risk	BUS
ARHA	Assiniboine Regional Health Authority (a Manitoba Regional Health Authority)	ORG
ARMA	Association for Record Managers & Administrators	IM
ASC	Access Service Coordinator	IM
ASC	Advanced Simulation and Computing	IT
ASC	Ambulatory Surgical Centre	ORG
ASCII	American Standard Code for Information Interchange	STD
ASP	Application Service Provider	IT
ASTM	American Society for Testing & Materials	STD
ASTM E31	American Society for Testing and Materials Committee E31 on	STD

ACRONYM	DEFINITION	DOMAIN
	Computerized Systems	
AT	Advanced Technology	IT
ATM	Account Technical Manager	BUS
ATM	Asynchronous Transfer Mode	IT
AVH	Annapolis Valley District Health Authority (a Nova Scotia Regional Health Authority)	ORG
AWOL	Absence Without Leave	CL

ACRONYM	DEFINITION	DOMAIN
B		
BAC	Budget at Completion	PM
BBS	Bulletin Board System	IT
BCP	Bar Code Printer	IT
BCP	Blood Chemistry Profile	CL
BCP	Bridge Control Protocol	IT
BCP	Business Continuity Plan(ning)	IM
BCWP	Budgeted Cost of Work Performed	PM
BI	Binary Input	IT
BI	Brain Injury	CL
BI	Business Intelligence	BUS
BIOS	Basic Input Output System	IT
BISDN	Broadband Integrated Services Digital Network	IT
BMP	Behavioral Medicine Program	ORG
BMP	Bit Map (A Windows file format for storing images)	IT
BoB	Best of Breed	IT
BoD	Board of Directors	ORG
BOT	Back Office Transformation	BUS

ACRONYM	DEFINITION	DOMAIN
bpi	Bits Per Inch	IT
BPI	Bytes Per Inch	IT
BPI	Business Process Improvement	BUS
BRHA	Burntwood Regional Health Authority (a Manitoba Regional Health Authority)	ORG
BSC	Balanced Scorecard	HIM
BSC	Block Sum Check	IT
BSI	British Standards Institute	STD

ACRONYM	DEFINITION	DOMAIN
C		
CA	Certification Authority	IT
CA	Certified Archivist	IM
CA	Conceptual Architecture	IT
CA	Control Account	PM
C&A	Coding and Abstracting	HIM
CAC	Canadian Advisory Committee	STD
CAC	Common Access Card	IT
CAC	Cost at Completion	PM
CACS	Comprehensive Ambulatory care Classification System	STD
CAEP	Canadian Association of Emergency Physicians	ORG
CAHIIM	Commission on Accreditation for Health Informatics and Information Management education (U.S.A.)	ORG
CAMH	Centre for Addiction and Mental Health	ORG
CAP	Client Assessment Protocol	CL
CAP	Community-Acquired Pneumonia	CL
CAP	Computer Access Protocol	IM
CAR	Canadian Association of Radiologists	ORG

ACRONYM	DEFINITION	DOMAIN
CAR	Computer-Assisted Retrieval	IM
CBDHA	Cape Breton District Health Authority (a Nova Scotia Regional Health Authority)	ORG
CC	Chronic Care	CL
CCAC	Community Care Access Centre	ORG
CCB	Change Control Board	PM
CCC	Clinical Care Classification	STD
CCC	Complex Continuing Care	CL
CCD	Continuity of Care Document (HL7)	STD
CCEP	Canadian Centre for Emergency Preparedness	ORG
CCHFA	Canadian Council on Health Facilities Accreditation	ORG
CCHIM	Canadian College of Health Information Management	ORG
CCHIT	Certification Commission for Healthcare Information Technology (USA)	ORG
CCHSE	Canadian College of Health Service Executives	ORG
CCI	Canadian Classification of health Interventions	STD
CCOW	Clinical Context Object Workgroup (HL7)	STD
CCR	Continuity of Care Record (ASTM)	STD

ACRONYM	DEFINITION	DOMAIN
CCRS	Continuing Care Reporting System (CIHI)	HIM
CD	Compact Disc	IT
CDA	Clinical Document Architecture (HL7)	STD
CDA	Canadian Diabetic Association	ORG
CDC	Center for Disease Control (Atlanta, USA)	ORG
CDHA	Capital District Health Authority (a Nova Scotia Regional Health Authority)	ORG
CDISC	Clinical Data Interchange Standards Consortium	STD
CDM	Chronic Disease Management	CL
CDM	Consent Directive Management	HIM
CDN	Canadian	BUS
CD-R	CD-Recordable	IT
CDR	Clinical Data Repository	HIM
CD-ROM	CD Read-Only Memory	IT
CD-RW	CD Re-Writable	IT
CDS	Clinical Decision Support	HIM
CDSS	Clinical Decision Support System	IT
CDT	Current Dental Terminology	STD
CDW	Clinical Data Warehouse	HIM

ACRONYM	DEFINITION	DOMAIN
CEN	Comite European de Normalisation	STD
CEO	Chief Executive Officer	BUS
CFO	Chief Financial Officer	BUS
CH	Capital Health (an Alberta Regional Health Authority)	ORG
CHA	Canada Health Act	LAW
CHA	Canadian Healthcare Association	ORG
CHAC	Catholic Health Association of Canada	ORG
CHAP	Comparison of Hospital Activity Program (CIHI)	HIM
CHC	Community Health Centre	ORG
CHDM	Conceptual Health Data Model (CIHI)	STD
CHE	Canadian Health Executive	BUS
CHES	Canadian Healthcare Engineering Society	ORG
CHI	Canada Health Infoway	ORG
CHI	Consolidated Health Informatics	ORG
CHIM	Certified Health Information Management professional	HIM
CHIMA	Canadian Health Information Management Association	ORG
CHIN	Community Health Information Network	ORG
CHIPP	Canadian Health Infostructure Partnership	ORG

C

ACRONYM	DEFINITION	DOMAIN
	Program	
CHP	Canadian Health Portal (CHI)	IM
CHR	Calgary Health Region (an Alberta Regional Health Authority)	ORG
CHR	Chinook Health Region (an Alberta Regional Health Authority)	ORG
CHRA	Canadian Health Records Association (now CHIMA)	ORG
CIHI	Canadian Institute for Health Information	ORG
CIHR	Canadian Institute for Health Research	ORG
CIO	Chief Information Officer	BUS
CIS	Clinical Information System	IT
CJRR	Canadian Joint Replacement Registry (CIHI)	HIM
CJNL	Canadian Journal of Nursing Leadership	CL
CKO	Chief Knowledge Officer	BUS
CLSI	Clinical and Laboratory Standards Institute	STD
CM	Chart Management	HIM
CM	Cluster Manager	IT
CM	Content Management	IM
CMA	Canadian Medical Association	ORG
CME	Continuing Medical Education	CL

ACRONYM	DEFINITION	DOMAIN
CMET	Common Message Element Type (HL7)	STD
CMG	Case-Mix Group	HIM
CMIO	Chief Medical Informatics Officer	BUS
CMO	Chief Medical Officer	BUS
CMOH	Chief Medical Officer of Health	BUS
CMPA	Canadian Medical Protective Association	ORG
CNA	Canadian Nurses Association	ORG
CNO	Chief Nursing Officer	BUS
COACH	Canada's Health Informatics Association	ORG
COBIT	Control OBjectives for Information and related Technology	IT
COM	Command (File name extension)	IT
COM	Communications	BUS
COM	Computer-Output to Microfilm	IM
COO	Chief Operating Officer	BUS
COLD/ERM	Computer Output to Laser Disk/ Enterprise Report Management	IT
CoP	Communities of Practice	BUS
COQ	Cost of Quality	PM
CORR	Canadian Organ Replacement Registry (CIHI)	HIM

C

ACRONYM	DEFINITION	DOMAIN
COS	Chief of Staff	ORG
COWs	Computers on Wheels	IT
CPHA	Canadian Public Health Association	ORG
CPI	Central Patient Index	HIM
CPI	Characters Per Inch	IM
CPI	Cost Performance Index	PM
CPM	Critical Path Method	PM
CPO	Chief Privacy Officer	ORG
CPOE	Computerized Provider Order Entry	IM
CPR	Computer-based Patient Record	HIM
CPRI	Computer-based Patient Record Institute	ORG
CPro	Client Profile	HIM
CPS	College of Physicians and Surgeons	ORG
CPS	Compendium of Pharmaceuticals and Specialties	CL
CPSI	Canadian Patient Safety Institute	ORG
CPU	Central Processing Unit	IT
CQI	Continuous Quality Improvement	BUS
CR	Client Registry	HIM
CR	Computed Radiology	CL

C

ACRONYM	DEFINITION	DOMAIN
CR	Concurrent Review	HIM
CRHA	Churchill RHA Inc. (a Manitoba Regional Health Authority)	ORG
CRIHA	Central Regional Integrated Health Authority [Central Health] (a Newfoundland and Labrador Regional Health Authority)	ORG
CRM	Certified Records Manager	IM
CRM	Clinical Risk Management	CL
CRM	Customer Relationship Management	BUS
CSA	Canadian Standards Association	ORG
CSHP	Canadian Society of Hospital Pharmacists	ORG
CSO	Chief Security Officer	BUS
CT	Clinical Trial	CL
CT	Communications Technology	IT
CT	Computerized Tomography	CL
CTAS	Canadian Triage Acuity Scale	CL
CTI	Computer–Telephone Integration	IT
CTI	Cycle Time Improvement	BUS
CTO	Chief Technology Officer	BUS
CV	Cost Variance	PM
CV	Curriculum Vitae	BUS

C

ACRONYM	DEFINITION	DOMAIN

ACRONYM	DEFINITION	DOMAIN
D		
DAD	Discharge Abstract Database (CIHI)	HIM
DASD	Direct Access Storage Device	IT
dB	Decibel	IT
DB	Data Base	IM
DBA	Database Administrator	IT
DBLC	Database Life Cycle	IT
DBMS	Database Management System	IT
DC	Data Centre	IT
DC	Daycare	CL
D/C	Discharge (*See* 'Disch')	CL
DCS	Daily Census Summary	HIM
DCWG	Data Consistency Working Group	HIM
DD	Data Dictionary	HIM
DDA	Document Disposal Act	HIM
DES	Data Element Standardization	IM
DES	Data Encryption Standards	STD
DFS	Distributed File System (Microsoft)	IT
DI	Data Integrity	HIM

ACRONYM	DEFINITION	DOMAIN
DI	Diagnostic Image/Diagnostic Imaging	CL
DIAMS	Data Issues and Actions Management System	IT
DICOM	Digital Imaging and Communication in Medicine	STD
DIS	Distributed Information System	IT
DIS	Draft International Standard	STD
DIS	Drug Information System	IT
Disch	Discharge (See 'D/C')	CL
DM	Diabetes Mellitus	CL
DM	Disaster Management	BUS
DM	Disease Management	CL
DM	Document Management	IM
DMC	Data Management Coordinator	HIM
DNKA	Did Not Keep Appointment	IM
DNS	Domain Name Server	IT
DOA	Dead On Arrival	CL
DOA	Denial of Access	IM
DOD	Department of Defense	ORG
DoD	Date of Death	HIM

ACRONYM	DEFINITION	DOMAIN
DoD	Day of Discharge	HIM
DPG	Day Procedure Group (CIHI)	HIM
DPI	Dots per Inch	IM
DQ	Data Quality	HIM
DQM	Data Quality Management	HIM
DQMF	Data Quality Management Framework	HIM
Dr.	Doctor	CL
DS	Decision Support	CL
DS	Digital Signature	IM
DSA	Digital Signature Algorithm	IT
DSM–IV–TR	Diagnostic and Statistical Manual of Mental Disorders, Fourth Revision, Text Revision	STD
DSP	Digital Signal Processor	IT
DSS	Decision Support System	IT
DSS	Digital Signature Service	IM
DSS	Distributed Software Systems	IT
D&T	Dictation & Transcription	HIM
D&T	Diagnosis & Treatment	CL
DTC	Diagnostic & Treatment Centre	ORG

ACRONYM	DEFINITION	DOMAIN
DTHR	David Thompson Health Region (an Alberta Regional Health Authority)	ORG
DTMF	Dual Tone Multi-Frequency	IT
DVD	Digital Versatile Disk	IT
DWA	Discharge Without Approval	CL

ACRONYM	DEFINITION	DOMAIN
E		
EAI	Electronic Architecture Integration	IT
EC	Executive Council / Executive Committee	BUS
EC	Extended Care	CL
ECH	East Central Health (an Alberta Regional Health Authority)	ORG
ECM	Electronic Content Management	IM
ECM	Enterprise Content Management	IM
ECPEWC	Expected Cost Per Equivalent Weighted Case	HIM
ECRM	Enterprise Content and Records Management	IM
ECU	Extended Care Unit	ORG
ED	Electronic Discovery	LAW
ED	Emergency Department (See 'ER')	ORG
EDI	Electronic Data Interchange	STD
EDIFACT	Electronic Data Interchange For Administration, Commerce and Transport (UN)	STD
EDM	Electronic Document Management	IM
EDM	Electronic Data Management	IM
EDM	Emergency Disaster Management	BUS

ACRONYM	DEFINITION	DOMAIN
EHC	Extended Health Coverage	BUS
EHR	Electronic Health Record	STD
EHR	Environmental Health Review	BUS
EHRA	EHR Architecture	STD
EHRi	Electronic Health Record infostructure	STD
EHRM	Electronic Health Record Management	HIM
EHRRA	Electronic Health Record Reference Architecture (ISO)	STD
EHR(s)	Electronic Health Record(s)	HIM
EHRS	Electronic Health Record System or Electronic Health Record Solution	IT
EI	Emotional Intelligence	BUS
EIM	Electronic Image Management	IM
EIM	Enterprise Information Management	IM
EIM	Enterprise Instant Messaging	IT
EIS	Executive Information System	IT
ELOS	Expected Length of Stay (CIHI)	HIM
ELR	Enterprise Location Registry	HIM
EMAR	Electronic Medication Administration Record	CL
EMI	Electromagnetic Interference	IT

ACRONYM	DEFINITION	DOMAIN
EMP	Emergency Measures Planning	BUS
EMPI	Enterprise(-wide) Master Person/Patient Index	HIM
eMPI	Electronic Master Patient Index	HIM
EMR	Electronic Mail Registration	IT
EMR	Electronic Medical Record	HIM
EMS	Electronic Medical Summary	HIM
EMS	Emergency Management System	IT
EMS	Emergency Medical Services	ORG
ENCODE-FM	Electronic Nomenclature and Classification of Disorders and Encounters for Family Medicine	STD
EPI	Electronic Patient Index	HIM
EPI	Enterprise Process Improvement	BUS
EPR	Electronic Patient Record	HIM
EPR	Employee Profile Record	BUS
EPR	Enterprise Provider Registry	HIM
ER	Emergency Room (See 'ED')	ORG
ERD	Entity Relationship Diagram	IT
ERIHA	Eastern Regional Integrated Health Authority (a Newfoundland and Labrador Regional Health Authority)	ORG

ACRONYM	DEFINITION	DOMAIN
ERM	Electronic Record Management	IM
ERM	Enterprise Report Management	IM
ERM	Enterprise Resource Management	BUS
ERMS	Electronic Record Management System	IT
e-Rx	Electronic Prescribing or "e-Script"	CL
ES	Encryption Service	IT
ES	Expert System	CL
ESA	Electronic Signature Authentication	HIM
ESA	Enterprise Services Architecture	IT
ESC	Executive Steering Committee	ORG
ETA	Electronic Transactions Act (British Columbia)	LAW
ETC	Emergency Trauma Centre	CL
ETC	Estimate to Complete	PM
EV	Earned Value	PM
EV	Expected Value	LAW

ACRONYM	DEFINITION	DOMAIN
F		
FAN	File Area Network	IT
FI	Federated Identifier	IM
FIMB	Finance and Information Management Branch (Ontario MoHLTC)	ORG
FIPA	(BC) Freedom of information and Privacy Association	ORG
FIPPA	Freedom of Information and Protection of Privacy Act	LAW
FN	Family Name	IM
FN	First Nation	ORG
FN	Function (keyboard key)	IT
FOI	Freedom of Information (Act)	LAW
FOI	Fibre Optic Interface	IT
FOIP	Freedom of Information and Protection of Privacy [Act] (Alberta, Saskatchewan, Ontario, Prince Edward Island)	LAW
FOIPPA	Freedom of Information and Protection of Privacy Act (British Columbia, Manitoba, Nova Scotia, PEI)	LAW
FHA	Fraser Health Authority (a British Columbia Regional Health Authority)	ORG
FTE	Full Time Equivalent	BUS

ACRONYM	DEFINITION	DOMAIN

ACRONYM	DEFINITION	DOMAIN
G		
GAL	Global Address List (Microsoft Outlook)	IM
GASHA	Guysborough Antigonish Strait Health Authority (a Nova Scotia Regional Health Authority)	ORG
GB	Gigabyte	IT
GB	Glass Break (physical security sensor)	BUS
GUI	Graphical User Interface (pronounced 'gooey')	IT
GMDN	Global Medical Device Nomenclature	STD

ACRONYM	DEFINITION	DOMAIN
H		
HA	Health Authority	ORG
HAA	Hospital Accountability Agreement	BUS
HAPS	Hospital Annual Planning Submission	BUS
HBAM	Health Based Allocation Model (Ontario LHINs)	BUS
HC	Health Canada	ORG
HC	Health Centre	ORG
HC	Home Care	ORG
HC	Huffman Coding (data compression)_	IT
HCA	Home Care Assessment	CL
HCA	Health Care Aide	CL
HCCSB	Home Care and Community Support Branch	ORG
HCFA	Health Care Financing Administration (USA, Department of Health and Human Services)	ORG
HCPRA	Health Care Public Relations Association of Canada	ORG
HCRS	Home Care Reporting System	IT
HEICS	Hospital Emergency Incident Command	BUS

ACRONYM	DEFINITION	DOMAIN
	System	
HFA	Home for the Aged	ORG
HFC	Hybrid Fiber/Coax(ial)	IT
HIA	Health Information Act (Alberta)	LAW
HIAL	Health Information Access Layer (Canada Health Infoway also refers to this as "EHRi common services")	IT
HIE	Health Information Exchange	STD
HIM	Hardware Interface Model	IT
HIM	Health Information Management	HIM
HIMAA	Health Information Management Association of Alberta	ORG
HIMAC	Health Information Management Advisory Committee	ORG
HIMSS	Health Information and Management Systems Society	ORG
HIN	Health-Info-Net	IT
HIN	Health Information Network	IT
HIN	Hemophilus Influenza	CL
HIPA	Health Information Protection Act (Saskatchewan)	LAW
HIPAA	Health Insurance Portability and Accountability Act of 1996 (USA)	LAW

ACRONYM	DEFINITION	DOMAIN
HIS	Health Information Services	IM
HIS	Hospital Information System	IT
HIS	Host Integration Server	IT
HISC	Health Information Standards Council (or Provincial Health Information Standards Committee)	ORG
HISP	Health Information Sciences Program (Douglas College, BC)	ORG
HISP	Health Infostructure Support Program	ORG
HIT	Health Information Technology	IT
HIT	Home Infusion Therapy	CL
HL7	Health Level Seven	STD
HMDB	Hospital Morbidity Data Base (CIHI)	HIM
HMHDB	Hospital Mental Health Data Base (CIHI)	HIM
HMR	Hazardous Material Report	IM
HMR	Hospital Medical Records	ORG
HMRI	Hospital Medical Records Institute (See CIHI)	ORG
HPDB	Hospital Personnel Data Base (CIHI)	IM
HP	Hewlett Packard	ORG
HPI	Health Policy Institute	ORG

ACRONYM	DEFINITION	DOMAIN
HPI	Health Provider Index	IM
HPI	History of Present Illness	CL
HRABC	Health Record Association of British Columbia	ORG
HRDC	Human Resources Development Canada	ORG
HRI	Health Resources Information	IM
HRM	Health Record Management	HIM
HRRC	Hospital Report Research Collaborative	ORG
HRT	Health Record Technician	HIM
HRT	Hormone Replacement Therapy	CL
HRT–IM	Health Results Team – Information Management (Ontario)	ORG
HSMR	Hospital Standardized Mortality Rate	HIM
HSS	Health Surveillance System	HIM
HSS	Host System Software	IT
HTML	Hypertext Markup Language	STD
HTTP	Hypertext Transport Protocol	STD
HTTPs	Hypertext Transport Protocol secured	STD
HuGN	Human Genome Nomenclature	STD

H

ACRONYM	DEFINITION	DOMAIN

ACRONYM	DEFINITION	DOMAIN
I		
IA	Information Architecture	IT
IA	Information Assurance	IM
IA	Interface Architect	IT
IA	Internal Audit	BUS
IC	Incoming Calls	IT
IC	Intensive Care	CL
IC	Intermediate Care	CL
IC	Inventory Control	BUS
ICD-9	International Classification of Diseases, 9th Revision (WHO)	STD
ICD-9-CM	International Classification of Diseases, 9th Revision, Clinical Modification (WHO)	STD
ICD-10-CA	International Classification of Diseases and Related Health Problems, 10th Revision, Canadian edition (WHO)	STD
ICD-10-PCS	International Classification of Diseases, 10th Revision, Procedure Coding System (WHO)	STD
ICD-O-3	International Classification of Diseases for Oncology, 3rd Edition (WHO)	STD
ICES	Institute for Clinical Evaluative Sciences (Ontario)	ORG

ACRONYM	DEFINITION	DOMAIN
ICES	International Credential Evaluation Service	ORG
ICF	Intermediate Care facility	ORG
ICF	International Classification on Functioning, Disability and Health (WHO)	STD
ICNP	International Classification for Nursing Practice	STD
ICPC	International Classification of Primary Care	STD
ICR	Intelligent Character Recognition	IM
ICRM	Institute of Certified Records Managers	ORG
ICT	Information and Communication Technologies	IT
ICT	Integrative Cancer Therapies	CL
ICU	Intensive Care Unit	CL
ID	Identification	IM
ID	Instructional Design	ORG
IDEA	International Data Encryption Algorithm	STD
IDN	Integrated Delivery Network	IT
IDP	Individual Development Plan	BUS
IDS	Integrated Delivery System	ORG

ACRONYM	DEFINITION	DOMAIN
IDS	Integrated Data Storage	IT
IDS	Interface Design Specification	IT
IEC	International Electrotechnical Commission	ORG
IEEE	Institute of Electrical and Electronics Engineers	ORG
iEHR	Interoperable Electronic Health Record	STD
IFB	Invitation for Bid	BUS
IFHRO	International Federation of Health Record Organizations	ORG
IHA	Interior Health Authority (a British Columbia Regional Health Authority)	ORG
IHE	Integrating the Healthcare Enterprise (USA)	ORG
IHE	Institute for Health Economics	ORG
IHE Canada	Integrating the Healthcare Enterprise Canada	ORG
IHSP	Integrated Health Service Plan	BUS
ILM	Information Lifecycle Management	IM
IM	Identity Management	IM
IM	Index Medicus	IM
IM	Information Management	IM

ACRONYM	DEFINITION	DOMAIN
IM	Instant Messaging	IT
IM	Internal Medicine	CL
IMIA	International Medical Informatics Association	ORG
IMS	Identity Management Service	IM
IMS	Incident Management System	IT
IOM	Infrastructure Optimization Model	IT
IOM	Installation and Operation Manual	BUS
IOM	Institute of Medicine; a body of the US National Institutes of Health	ORG
IP	Internet Protocol	STD
IP	Intellectual Property	BUS
IPO	Input/Processing/Output	IT
IPO	Integrated Provider Organization	ORG
IPBA	Integrated Population Based Allocation	HIM
IPC	Information & Privacy Commissioner	BUS
IPC	Information Protection and Control	IT
IPPH	Institute of Population and Public Health	ORG
IPS	Identity Protection Service	IM
IRA	Incomplete Record Area	HIM

ACRONYM	DEFINITION	DOMAIN
IRA	Internet Routing Address	IT
IRB	Institutional Review Board	BUS
IRHA	Interlake Regional Health Authority (Manitoba Regional Health Authority)	ORG
IRIS	Immunization Record Information System	IT
IRIS	Incident Reporting Information System	IT
IRIS	Integrated Records & Information System	IM
IRR	Information Request Response	IM
IRR	Internal Rate of Return	BUS
IS	Information Security	IT
IS	Information Systems	IT
IS	In Service	BUS
IS	Inventory or Systems	CL
ISACA	Information Systems Audit and Control Association	ORG
ISBN	International Standard Book Number	STD
ISDN	Integrated Services Digital Network	IT
ISO	Internal Standards Organization (United Nations)	STD
ISO/TC215	International Standards Organization Technical Committee 215 (on	STD

ACRONYM	DEFINITION	DOMAIN
	healthcare informatics)	
ISO/IEC	International Standards Organization/ International Electrotechnical Commission	STD
ISS	Information Security Services	IT
ISS	Injury Severity Score	CL
ISS	Isotonic Saline Solution	CL
IT	Information Technology	IT
ITGI	IT Governance Institute	ORG
IVR	Interactive Voice Recognition	IT
IVR	Intelligent Voice Response	IT

ACRONYM	DEFINITION	DOMAIN
J		
JCAHO	Joint Commission on Accreditation of Healthcare Organizations (USA)	ORG
JPEG	Joint Photographic Experts Group	STD
JPPC	Joint Policy & Planning Committee	ORG
K		
Kbps	Kilobits per second	IT
KM	Knowledge Management	IM
KMS	Knowledge Management System	IT
KT	Kidney Transplantation	CL
KT	Knowledge Translation	IM
KTA	Knowledge to Action	IM

ACRONYM	DEFINITION	DOMAIN
L		
LAN	Local Area Network	IT
LDAP	Lightweight Directory Access Protocol	IT
LDMP	Local Data Management Partnership (Ontario)	ORG
LE	Life expectancy	CL
LGRIHA	Labrador–Grenfell Regional Integrated Health Authority (a Newfoundland and Labrador Regional Health Authority)	ORG
LHIN	Local Health Integration Network (Ontario)	ORG
LIS	Laboratory Information System	IT
LIS	Learning information System	IT
LIS	Legacy Information Systems	IT
LIS	Library & Information Services	IM
LOA	Leave of Absence	BUS
LOINC®	Logical Observation Identifier Names and Codes	STD
LOS	Length of Stay	HIM
LOS	Loss of Signal	IT
LTC	Lap Top Computer	IT
LTC	Long Term Care	CL

L

ACRONYM	DEFINITION	DOMAIN
LTCF	Long Term Care facility	ORG
LTD	Long Term Disability	CL
LWBS	Left Without Being Seen	CL

ACRONYM	DEFINITION	DOMAIN
M		
MAC	Medical Advisory Committee	ORG
MAC	Maximum Allowable Cost	BUS
MAC	Message Authentication Code	IT
Mac	Macintosh (slang for Apple Computer)	IT
M/A/C	Move/Add/Change	IT
MAN	Metropolitan Area Network	IT
MAR	Memory Address Register	IT
MAR	Medication Administration Record	CL
MAR	Multiple Antibiotic Resistant	CL
MaRS0	Medical and Related Sciences	CL
MB	Megabyte	IT
MB	Memory Buffer	IT
MB	Myoglobin	CL
MBO	Management by Objectives	BUS
MCC	Major Clinical Category (CIHI)	HIM
MCC	Mobile Country Code	IT
MDC	Medical Day Care	ORG
MDC	Mood Disorders Clinic	ORG

ACRONYM	DEFINITION	DOMAIN
MDS	Minimum Data Set	HIM
MEDLINE	MEDical literature, analysis and retrieval system onLINE	IM
MedRec	Medical Record	HIM
MedRec	Medication Reconciliation	CL
MFIPPA	Municipal Freedom of Information and Protection of Privacy Act (Ontario)	LAW
MHIMA	Manitoba Health Information Management Association	ORG
MIB	IEEE Committee P1073, Medical Information Bus	STD
MICR	Magnetic Ink Character Recognition	IT
MIM	Message Information Model (HL7)	IT
MIS	Management Information System	IT
MOH	Medical Officer of Health	ORG
MoH	Ministry of Health	ORG
MoHLTC	Ministry of Health and Long-Term Care	ORG
MOLAP	Multidimensional OnLine Analytical Processing	IM
MOU	Memorandum of Understanding	BUS
MoU	Minutes of User	IT
MPEG	Moving Pictures Expert Group	STD

ACRONYM	DEFINITION	DOMAIN
MPI	Master Patient Index	HIM
MPI	Multipage Interface (web)	IT
MPI	Multiservice Packet Interface	IT
MRDx	Most Responsible Diagnosis (CIHI)	HIM
MRI	Medical Resonance Imaging	CL
MRI	Medical Records Institute (USA)	ORG
MRP	Most Responsible Physician	HIM
MSO	Management Service Organization	BUS
MT	Magnetic Tape	IT
MT	Massage Therapist	CL
MT	Medical Technologist (Lab)	CL
MT	Medical Transcriptionist	HIM
MTSO	Medical Transcription Service Organization	BUS

ACRONYM	DEFINITION	DOMAIN
N		
NACRS	National Ambulatory Care Reporting System (CIHI)	HIM
NANDA International Taxonomy	North American Nursing Diagnosis Association International Taxonomy	HIM
NAS	Network Access Server	IT
NAS	Network Attached Storage	IT
NBHIMA	New Brunswick Health information Management Association	ORG
NCAD	National Clinical Administrative Databases (at CIHI)	HIM
NCITS	International Committee for Information Technology Standards	STD
NCPDP	National Council for Prescription Drug Programs (USA)	STD
NEAT	Non-Emergency Ambulance Transport	BUS
NEC	Not Elsewhere Classified	HIM
NeCST	National Electronic Claims STandard (CHI)	STD
NEHA	North Eastman Health Authority (a Manitoba Regional Health Authority)	ORG
NGS	National Grouping System (CIHI)	HIM

ACRONYM	DEFINITION	DOMAIN
NGS	Next Generation Systems	IT
NH	Nursing Home	ORG
NHEX	National Health Expenditure Database (CIHI)	HIM
NHIN	National Health Information Network (USA)	ORG
NHS	National Health Service (UK)	ORG
NI	Needs Improvement	BUS
NI	Network Interface	IT
NI	Nursing Informatics	IT
NIC	Network Interface Cards	IT
NIC	Nursing Interventions Classification	STD
NIH	National Institutes of Health (USA)	ORG
NLHIMA	Newfoundland and Labrador Health Information Management Association	ORG
NLHR	Northern Lights Health Region (an Alberta Regional Health Authority)	ORG
NLP	Natural Language Processing	IT
NLP	Neuro-Linguistic Programming	CL
NMDS	Nursing Minimum Data Set	HIM
NML	Network Management Layer	IT

ACRONYM	DEFINITION	DOMAIN
NNI	Network to Network Interface	IT
NOC	Nursing Outcomes Classification	STD
NOS	Network Operating System	IT
NOS	Not otherwise specified	HIM
NPDB	National Physicians Data Base (CIHI)	HIM
NPDUIS	National Prescription Drug Utilization Information System (CIHI)	HIM
NPHS	National Population Health Survey (CIHI)	HIM
NRHA	NOR–MAN Regional Health Authority (a Manitoba Regional Health Authority)	ORG
NRS	National Rehabilitation Reporting System	HIM
NRS	Name Resolution Server	IT
NRS	Network Routing Solution	IT
NS	Name Server	IT
NS	Nervous System	CL
NS	No Show	HIM
NS	Normal Saline	CL
NSHIMA	Nova Scotia Health Information	ORG

ACRONYM	DEFINITION	DOMAIN
	Management Association	
NSS	National Standards System	STD
NTP	Network Time Protocol	IT
NTP	Nurse Transition Program	ORG
NTR	National Trauma Registry (CIHI)	HIM

ACRONYM	DEFINITION	DOMAIN
O		
OACCAC	Ontario Association of Community Care Access Centres	ORG
OASIS	Outcomes and Assessment Information Set	HIM
OBS	Obstetrics	CL
OBS	Organizational Breakdown Structure	PM
OCCPS/ CCRS	Ontario Chronic Care Patient System/Continuing Care Reporting System	HIM
OCR	Optical Character Recognition	IM
ODA	Open Document Architecture	IT
ODP	Open Distributed Processing	STD
ODP	Optical Disk Playback	IM
OHCAS	Ontario Home Care Administration System	HIM
OHCIDD	Ontario Health Client Identification Data Dictionary	HIM
OHIH	Office of Health and the Information Highway	ORG
OHIMA	Ontario Health Information Management Association	ORG
OHISC	Ontario Health Informatics Standards Council	ORG

ACRONYM	DEFINITION	DOMAIN
OH&S	Occupational Health and Safety	BUS
OID	Object IDentifier	STD
OIPC	Office of the Information and Privacy Commissioner	ORG
OLAP	OnLine Analytical Processing	IT
OLTCCS	Ontario Long Term Care Classification System	HIM
OLTP	OnLine Transaction Processing	IT
OMG	Object Management Group	IT
OMHRS	Ontario Mental Health Reporting System	HIM
OODB	Object–Oriented Data Base	IM
OPD	Organizational Process Definition	BUS
OPD	Out Patient Department	ORG
OR	Object Recognition	IT
OR	Operating Room	CL
OR	Operational Review	ORG
ORA	Organizational Readiness Assessment	ORG
ORBC	Operating Room Benchmarking Collaborative	ORG
OSHA	Occupational Safety and Health Administration (USA)	ORG

O

ACRONYM	DEFINITION	DOMAIN
OWL	Web Ontology Language (3 sublanguages) OWL Lite, OWL DL, OWL Full)	STD

ACRONYM	DEFINITION	DOMAIN
P		
P&S	Privacy & Security	IM
PAC-10	ICD-10 based Relative Cost Weights, PAC-10 (Ontario)	HIM
PACS	Picture Archiving and Communication System	IT
PACU	Post-Anesthetic Care Unit	CL
PAR	Problem Analysis Report	BUS
PARR	Post-Anesthetic Recovery Room	CL
PBX	Private Branch Exchange	IT
PC	Percent Complete	PM
PC	Personal Computer	IT
PC	Postal Code	IM
PCHR	Peace Country Health (an Alberta Regional Health Authority)	ORG
PCI	Patient Care Information	IM
pCLOCD	pan-Canadian Laboratory Observation Code Database	STD
PCP	Primary Care Physician	CL
pCSG	pan-Canadian Standards Group	STD

ACRONYM	DEFINITION	DOMAIN
PDA	Personal Digital Assistant	IT
PDEP	Physician Documentation Expert Panel (Ontario)	ORG
PDF	Portable Document Format	STD
PDSA	Plan-Do-Study-Act cycle	BUS
PERT	Program Evaluation and Review Technique	BUS
PETs	Privacy Enhancing Technologies	IT
PHI	Personal Health Information	HIM
PHI	Protected Health Information	HIM
PHIA	Personal Health Information Act (Manitoba)	LAW
PHIN	Public Health Information Network	IT
PHIPA	Personal Health Information Protection Act (Ontario)	LAW
PHPDB	Provincial Health Planning Database	HIM
PHR	Palliser Health Region (an Alberta Regional Health Authority)	ORG
PHR	Personal Health Record	HIM
PHS	Public Health Surveillance	HIM

ACRONYM	DEFINITION	DOMAIN
PHSA	(The) Provincial Health Services Authority (a British Columbia Regional Health Authority)	ORG
PIA	Privacy Impact Assessment	HIM
PID	Public IDentifier	IM
PIPA	Personal Information Protection Act (Alberta, British Columbia)	LAW
PIPEDA	Personal Information Protection and Electronic Documents Act (Canada, Federal)	LAW
PIS	Pharmacy Information System	IT
PKC	Public Key Certificate	IT
PKI	Public Key Infrastructure	IT
PM	Project Management	PM
PM	Project Manager	PM
PMBoK®	Project Management Body of Knowledge	PM
PMI®	Project Management Institute	PM
PMIS	Project Management Information System	IT
PMO	Project Management Office	PM
PMP®	Project Management Professional	PM

ACRONYM	DEFINITION	DOMAIN
PMS	Pharmacy Management System	IT
PMS	Practice Management System	IT
PO	Privacy Office	HIM
PO	Phone Order	CL
p.o.	per os (by mouth)	CL
POC	Point-of-Care	CL
POC	Proof of Concept	PM
POMR	Problem-Oriented Medical Record	HIM
POS	Palm Operating System	IT
POS	Point-of-Service	CL
POS	Positive	CL
POSSID	POS (Point-of-service) System Instance Identifier	IM
PPeAT	Professional Practice e-learning and Assessment Tool (CHIMA)	HIM
PPH	Provincial Psychiatric Hospital	ORG
PPIA	Protection of Personal Information Act (New Brunswick)	LAW
PR	Payroll	BUS
PR	Peer Review	CL

ACRONYM	DEFINITION	DOMAIN
PR	Print (command)	IT
PR	Provider Registry	HIM
PRC	Packed Red Cells	CL
PRC	Physician Record Completion	HIM
PRHA	Parkland Regional Health Authority (a Manitoba Regional Health Authority)	ORG
PRISM International	Professional Records and information Services Management International	ORG
PSA	Power Supply Adapter	IT
PSA	Privacy Security Architecture	STD
Pseudo ID	Pseudonymous IDentifier	IM
PSW	Personal Support Worker	ORG
PV	Planned Value	PM
PV	Patient Visit	IM

ACRONYM	DEFINITION	DOMAIN
Q		
QA	Quantitative Analysis	HIM
QA	Quality Assurance	BUS
QC	Quality Control	PM
QI	Quality Indicators	BUS
QI	Quality Improvement	BUS
QoS	Quality of Service	BUS

ACRONYM	DEFINITION	DOMAIN
R		
RA	Readiness Assessment (Also see ORA)	ORG
RA	Regional Anesthetic	CL
RA	Registry Administrator	HIM
RA	Remote Access	IT
RACI [chart]	Responsible, Accountable, Consulted or Informed	IM
RAI	Resident Assessment Instrument	CL
RAID	Redundant Arrays of Independent (formerly 'Inexpensive') Disks	IT
RAI–HC	Resident Assessment Instrument – Home Care	CL
RAM	Random Access Memory	IT
RAM	Responsibility Assignment Matrix	PM
RAS	Reliability, Availability and Serviceability	IT
RB	Radio Button	IT
RB	Reciprocal Billing	BUS
RBAC	Role–Based Access Control	IM
RBRVS	Resource–Based Relative Value Scale	PM
RBS	Resource Breakdown Structure	PM
RBS	Risk Breakdown Structure	PM
RC	Record Control	HIM

ACRONYM	DEFINITION	DOMAIN
RC	Remote Client	IT
RC	Root Cause	PM
RCF	Remote Call Forwarding	IT
RCF	Residential Care Facility	ORG
RCMP	Royal Canadian Mounted Police	ORG
RCPSC	Royal College of Physicians and Surgeons of Canada	ORG
RDF	Record Definition Field	IT
RDF	Resource Development Framework	IT
RECU	Rehabilitation (Rehab) Extended Care Unit	ORG
RFE	Reason For Encounter	CL
RFE	Request for Enhancement	IT
RFE	Request for Estimate	BUS
RFI	Request for Information (purchasing)	BUS
RFI	Request for Information (release of information)	HIM
RFID	Radio Frequency IDentification	IT
RFP	Request For Proposal	BUS
RFQ	Request For Qualifications	BUS
RFQ	Request for Quotation	BUS
RHACM	Regional Health Authority – Central Manitoba Inc.	ORG

R

ACRONYM	DEFINITION	DOMAIN
RHAM	Regional Health Authorities of Manitoba	ORG
RIM	Record and Information Management	HIM
RIM	Reference Information Model (HL7)	STD
RIS	Radiology Information System	IT
RIW	Resource Intensity Weight	HIM
RJ	Registered jack	IT
RLS	Record Locator Service	IM
Rls	Release	IT
RM	Record Management	HIM
RM	Risk Management	CL, PM
RN	Random Number	IM
RN	Registered Nurse	CL
RN	Release Note	IT
RNDB	Registered Nurses Data Base (CIHI)	HIM
R/O	Rule Out	CL
ROE	Return on Equity	BUS
ROI	Release of Information	HIM
ROI	Return on Investment	BUS
ROLAP	Relational OnLine Analytical Processing	IM
ROM	Range of Motion	CL

R

ACRONYM	DEFINITION	DOMAIN
ROM	Read Only Memory	IM
ROM	Rupture of Membrane	CL
RM	Record Management	HIM
RP	Record Processing	HIM
RP	Release Packet	IT
RPN	Registered Practical Nurse	CL
RRS	Record Retention Schedule	IM
RUG	Representatives User Group	IT
RUG	Resource User Group	HIM
RUG-III	Resource Utilization Groups, Version III	STD

ACRONYM	DEFINITION	DOMAIN
S		
SAD	Seasonal Affective Disorder	CL
SAD	Street ADdress	IM
SAD	System Administration	IT
SAD	System Analysis and Design	IT
SAN	Storage Area Network	IT
SARS	Severe Acute Respiratory Syndrome	CL
SARV	Small Area Rate Variation	HIM
SAS	Statistical Analysis Software	HIM
SC	Standards Collaborative	ORG
SC	Steering Committee	ORG
SCC	Standards Council of Canada	ORG
SCCC	Standards Collaborative Coordinating Committee	ORG
SCSC	Standards Collaborative Strategic committee	ORG
SCWG	Standards Collaborative Working Group	ORG
SDC	Sleep Disorder Clinic	ORG
SDC	Software Development Centre	IT
SDC	Surgical Day Care	ORG

ACRONYM	DEFINITION	DOMAIN
SDLC	System Development Life Cycle	IT
SDM	Semantic Data Model	IT
SDM	Substitute Decision Maker	CL
SDO	Scheduled Day Off	BUS
SDO	Standards Development Organization	STD/ORG
SDS	Same Day Surgery (CIHI)	ORG
SDS	Software Design Specification	IT
SES	Socio-Economic Status	IM
SEH	South Eastman Health/Santé Sud-Est Inc. (a Manitoba Regional Health Authority)	ORG
SGC	Server Gateway Control	IT
SGC	Standard Geographical Classifications (Statistics Canada)	STD
SHIMA	Saskatchewan Health Information Management Association	ORG
SIG	Secure Internet Gateway	IT
SIG	Special Interest Group	ORG
SIP	Session Initiation Protocol	IT
SLA	Service Level Agreement	BUS
SLP	Service Location Protocol	IT
SLP	Speech Language Pathology	CL

ACRONYM	DEFINITION	DOMAIN
SMBI	Standards Management & Business Integration (Secretariat of OHISC)	ORG
SME	Subject Matter Expert	BUS
SMO	Server Management Objects	IT
SMO	Standards Maintenance Organization	STD/ ORG
SMTP	Simple Mail Transfer Protocol	STD
SNA	System Network Architecture	IT
SNF	Skilled Nursing Facility	ORG
SNODENT	Systemized Nomenclature of Dentistry	STD
SNOMED	Systemized Nomenclature of Human and Veterinary Medicine	STD
SNOMED CT	Systemized Nomenclature of Medicine; Clinical Terminology	STD
SOA	Sarbanes Oxley Act (USA)	LAW
SOA	Statement of Accounts	BUS
SOA	Service–Oriented Architecture	IT
SOC	Service Order Code	IT
SOW	Scope of Work	PM
SOW	Statement of Work	PM
SPSS	Statistical Package for Social Sciences	IM
SQL	Specified Quality Level	BUS

ACRONYM	DEFINITION	DOMAIN
SQL	Structured Query Language	IT
SSL	Secure Sockets Layer	IT
STC	Statistics Canada	ORG
STD	Sexually Transmitted Disease	CL
STD	Short Term Disability	CL
STD	Standard	STD
STP	Secure Transfer Protocol	IT
STP	Shielded Twisted Pair	IT
SV	Sacral Vertebrae	CL
SV	Schedule Variance	PM
SWND	South West Nova District Health Authority (a Nova Scotia Regional Health Authority)	ORG
SWOT	Strengths, Weaknesses, Opportunities and Threats (analysis)	BUS

ACRONYM	DEFINITION	DOMAIN
T		
TADB	Therapeutic Abortion Database (CIHI)	HIM
TAG	Technical Advisory Group	IT
TAG	Technical Architecture Group (CHI)	IT
TAO	Telehealth Association of Ontario	ORG
TAWPI	The Association for Work Process Improvement	ORG
TB	Terabyte	IT
TB	Tuberculosis	CL
TC	Target Completion date	PM
TC	Technical Committee (CHI)	IT
TC	Telecommunications Closet	IT
TCP	Transmission Control Protocol	IT
TCP/IP	Transmission Control Protocol/Internet Protocol	STD
TelCom	Telecommunications	IT
TH	Telehealth	IT
TH	Thursday	IM
TH	Trojan Horse	IT
T&M	Time and Material	BUS

ACRONYM	DEFINITION	DOMAIN
TQM	Total Quality Management	BUS
TMN	Telecommunications Management Network	IT
TRA	Threat and Risk Assessment	BUS
TS	Time Stamp (See TSC)	IM
TSC	Technical Sub-Committee	ORG
TSC	Technical Support Centre	ORG
TSC	Time Stamp Counter	IT
TSSIT	Technical Security Standard for Information Technology	STD
TTP	Technology Transfer Program	IT
TTP	Time Triggered Protocol	IT
TTP	Trusted Third Party	IM

ACRONYM	DEFINITION	DOMAIN
U		
UAS	User Authentication Service	IM
UDSMR	Unified Data System for Medical Rehabilitation (USA)	HIM
UHDDS	Uniform Hospital Discharge Data Set	HIM
UM	User Manual	IT
UM	User Module	IT
UM	Utilization Management	CL
UMDNS	Universal Medical Device Nomenclature System	STD
UML	Unified Modeling Language	STD
UMLS	Unified Medical Language System	STD
UMNO	Utilization Management Network of Ontario	ORG
UN	United Nations	ORG
UPI	Unique Personal Identifier	HIM
UPI	User Program Interface	IT
UPIN	Unique Physician Identification Number	HIM
UPS	Uninterrupted Power Source/supply	IT
UR	User Requirement	IT
UR	Uterine Rupture	CL

ACRONYM	DEFINITION	DOMAIN
UR	Utilization Review	HIM
URI	Uniform Resource Indicator	IT
URL	Uniform Resource Locator	IT
USHIK	United States Health Information Knowledgebase	IM
UTP	Unshielded Twisted Pair	IT

ACRONYM	DEFINITION	DOMAIN
V		
VCHA	Vancouver Coastal Health Authority (a British Columbia Regional Health Authority)	ORG
VIHA	Vancouver Island Health Authority (a British Columbia Regional Health Authority)	ORG
VLAN	Virtual Local Area Network	IT
VoIP	Voice over Internet Protocol	IT
VOR	Vendor of Record	BUS
VOR	Vestibulo–Ocular Reflex	CL
VPN	Virtual Private Network	IT

ACRONYM	DEFINITION	DOMAIN
W		
W3C	World Wide Web Consortium	ORG
WAN	Wide Area Network	IT
WBS	Work Breakdown Structure	PM
WEDI	Workgroup for Electronic Data Interchange (USA)	ORG
WERS	Web Enabled Reporting System	IT
WG	Working Group	ORG
WHIC	Western Health Information Collaborative	ORG
WHIC	Wizard for Hospital Indicator Calculation (WHIC tool of the Hospital Report Research Collaborative, Ontario)	HIM
WHO	World Health Organization	ORG
WIIFM	What's in it for me?	ORG
WLAN	Wireless Local Area Network	IT
WRHA	Winnipeg Regional Health Authority (a Manitoba Regional Health Authority)	ORG
WRIHA	Western Regional Integrated Health Authority (a Newfoundland and Labrador Regional Health Authority)	ORG
WSA	Web Services Architecture	IT
WTIS	Wait Time Information System	IT

ACRONYM	DEFINITION	DOMAIN
WTS	Wait Time Strategy	CL
WYSIWYG	What you see is what you get	IT

ACRONYM	DEFINITION	DOMAIN
X		
XAD	Extended ADdress	IM
XML	Extensible Markup Language	STD

ACRONYM	DEFINITION	DOMAIN
Y		

ACRONYM	DEFINITION	DOMAIN
Z		

PUBLICATION ORDER FORM

PUBLICATION	PRICE	QUANTITY	TOTAL
EHR Glossary	$34.50		
EHR Acronyms	$22.50		
EHR Retention Schedules (Pre-Order for Winter 2008)	$37.50		
SUBTOTAL			
GST (5% on Subtotal)			
Cdn Shipping & Handling Charge $9.95 *FREE SHIPPING on orders with Subtotal over $50.00*			
GRAND TOTAL			

Name & Title	☐ Cheque enclosed (Payable to e-HRM Consulting)
Organization	☐ Bill my Organization PO#_____ (Books shipped when payment rec'd)
Street Address	☐ Bill my VISA / MasterCard (circle one) Account Number below: _____
City, Province, Postal Code	
Phone	Expiry Date
Fax	Signature
e-Mail	(Your Credit Card bill will reflect a charge to *e-HRM Consulting*)

e**HRM** Consulting Inc
Health Record Management for the future

eMail: ehrm@telus.net

Please use subject line: Publication Order when ordering by eMail

Watch for More Titles to Come